Start Your Own Consulting Business: A Step-by-Step Guide to Success

Content

- Choosing a location, setting up equipment, and creating a professional workspace

8. Networking and Marketing

   - Building relationships and promoting your services to potential clients

9. Establishing Your Rates and Packages

   - Determining your fees and creating flexible packages for clients

10. Hiring and Managing Staff

    - Building a team and managing employees for growth and success

11. Financial Planning and Budgeting

    - Understanding your financial needs and creating a budget for your business

12. Securing Funding

    - Exploring options for funding and securing financing for your business

13. Understanding Legal Issues

    - Navigating contracts, taxes, and other legal considerations for your business

14. Building a Strong Network of Partners

- Collaborating with other businesses and building strategic partnerships

15. Utilizing Technology and Tools

    - Implementing technology and tools to streamline processes and increase efficiency

16. Staying Up-to-Date with Industry Trends

    - Keeping abreast of changes in the industry and adapting your services accordingly

17. Providing Excellent Customer Service

    - Building trust and maintaining relationships with clients

18. Measuring Your Success

    - Tracking and measuring your success to make informed decisions for growth

19. Continuously Improving Your Services

    - Evaluating your services and making necessary improvements for continued success

20. Maintaining a Healthy Work-Life Balance

    - Balancing work and personal life to avoid burnout and ensure sustainability

21. Building a Strong Online Presence

- Developing a strong online presence through website, social media, and other digital channels

22. Managing Your Reputation

- Protecting and enhancing your reputation through positive relationships and ethical practices

23. Growing Your Business

- Strategies for expanding your services and reaching new markets

24. Staying Organized and Productive

- Implementing systems and tools to stay organized and productive

25. Building Strong Client Relationships

- Establishing strong relationships with clients to foster loyalty and repeat business

26. Keeping Up with Competition

- Understanding the competitive landscape and differentiating your services

27. Expanding Your Services

- Offering new and innovative services to stay ahead of the competition

28. Building a Strong Referral Network

- Encouraging referrals and leveraging word-of-mouth marketing

29. Diversifying Your Business

- Exploring new opportunities and diversifying your business for stability and growth

30. Utilizing Social Media and Online Marketing

- Leveraging social media and online marketing to reach new customers

31. Creating a Strong Marketing Plan

- Developing a comprehensive marketing plan to promote your services

32. Building Relationships with Industry Leaders

- Networking and building relationships with industry leaders to gain recognition and exposure

33. Becoming an Authority in Your Field

- Establishing yourself as an expert in your field through speaking engagements, writing, and other Publications

34. Keeping Your Business Ethical

- Maintaining high ethical standards and building a reputation for integrity

35. Managing Client Expectations

- Setting clear expectations and communicating effectively with clients to manage expectations

36. Staying Focused on Your Goals

- Remaining focused on your goals and avoiding distractions for continued success

37. Developing a Strong Work Culture

- Building a positive and productive work culture for your team and clients

38. Maintaining a Growth Mindset

- Adopting a growth mindset and continuously learning and improving for success

39. Staying Adaptable and Resilient

- Being adaptable and resilient in the face of challenges and change

40. Celebrating Your Success

- Celebrating your achievements and recognizing the hard work and dedication it took to get there.

Chapter 1

Introduction to Consulting

Congratulations on taking the first step towards starting your own consulting business! In this chapter, we'll provide an overview of what consulting is, why you might want to start your own consulting business, and what you can expect from the journey ahead.

What is Consulting?

Consulting is a professional service that provides expert advice and assistance to organizations and individuals in a specific area of expertise. Consultants are hired to help businesses and individuals solve problems, improve processes, and achieve their goals.

Consulting can encompass a wide range of areas, including management, finance, marketing, technology, and human resources. Some common examples of consulting services include strategic planning, market research, organizational design, and process improvement.

Why Start Your Own Consulting Business?

Starting your own consulting business can be a rewarding and fulfilling experience, as you have the opportunity to help others while also pursuing your own career goals. Here are a few reasons why you might consider starting your own consulting business:

- Flexibility: As a consultant, you have the flexibility to set your own schedule and work from anywhere. You can choose the projects you work on and the clients you work with, allowing you to create a work-life balance that works for you.

- Independence: By starting your own business, you have the opportunity to be your own boss and make your own decisions. You're in control of your work, your clients, and your income.

- Expertise: If you have extensive knowledge and experience in a particular field, starting your own consulting business allows you to leverage that expertise and make a real impact on the lives of others.

- Potential for High Earnings: Consulting can be a lucrative career, especially as you gain experience and build your reputation. With the right marketing and networking efforts, you can grow your business and increase your income over time.

What You Can Expect from the Journey Ahead

Starting a consulting business is not a quick or easy process, but it can be an incredibly rewarding experience. Here's what you can expect from the journey ahead:

- Learning: You'll need to learn about various aspects of starting a business, such as market research, business planning, legal requirements, and financial management. This will require time, effort, and a willingness to learn and grow.

- Hard Work: Starting a business is hard work, and there will be ups and downs along the way. You'll need to be prepared to put in the time and effort required to make your business successful.

- Challenges: There will be challenges along the way, such as finding clients, managing finances, and dealing with competition. You'll need to be resilient and adaptable to overcome these challenges and succeed in the long term.

- Support: Starting a business can be lonely, but it's important to remember that you're not alone. Seek out support from family, friends, and other business owners who can provide advice and guidance along the way.

- Satisfaction: Despite the challenges, starting a consulting business can be incredibly satisfying. You have the opportunity to make a real impact on the lives of others and help businesses achieve their goals.

In conclusion, starting your own consulting business can be a challenging but rewarding journey. By taking the time to understand what consulting is, why you might want to start your own business, and what you can expect from the journey ahead, you'll be well on your way to success.

In the next chapter, we'll dive deeper into defining your niche and identifying the area of expertise you want to focus on in your consulting business. Stay tuned!

Chapter 2

Defining Your Niche

Now that you have a general understanding of what consulting is and why you might want to start your own consulting business, it's time to start thinking about your niche. Your niche is the specific area of expertise that you'll focus on in your consulting business.

Why Define Your Niche?

Defining your niche is an important step in the process of starting your own consulting business. There are several reasons why it's important to define your niche, including:

- Increased Expertise: By focusing on a specific area, you'll have the opportunity to become an expert in that field. This increased expertise will help you differentiate yourself from others and position you as a go-to consultant in your niche.

- Improved Marketing: Focusing on a specific niche will make it easier to target your marketing efforts and attract the right clients. When you know your niche, you can create a marketing message that resonates with your ideal clients and helps you stand out from the competition.

- Increased Profitability: By focusing on a specific niche, you'll be able to charge premium prices for your services. Clients are often willing to pay more for experts in their field, so by focusing on a specific area, you'll be able to increase your profitability.

How to Define Your Niche

Defining your niche can seem daunting, but it doesn't have to be. Here are some steps you can take to help you define your niche:

1. Assess Your Skills and Interests: Think about your skills and interests and what you're passionate about. What are you knowledgeable about and enjoy doing? Consider the areas where you have the most experience and expertise.

2. Research the Market: Research the market to see what areas of consulting are in demand and what areas are underserved. Look for gaps in the market that you can fill with your skills and expertise.

3. Identify Your Ideal Client: Who do you want to work with? Who are the clients you enjoy working with the most? Identifying your ideal client will help you focus your niche and target your marketing efforts.

4. Evaluate Your Competition: Take a look at your competition to see what they're offering and what they're not offering. This will give you a better understanding of the market and help you determine how you can differentiate yourself.

5. Test Your Niche: Before you fully commit to your niche, it's a good idea to test it out. Offer your services to a few clients in your target market and see how it goes.

This will give you an opportunity to refine your niche and make sure it's a good fit for you.

Once you've completed these steps, you'll have a clearer idea of your niche and the area of expertise you want to focus on in your consulting business.

The Importance of Staying Focused

Once you've defined your niche, it's important to stay focused and not spread yourself too thin. When you're starting out, it's tempting to take on any client that comes your way, but this can be detrimental to your business.

By staying focused on your niche, you'll be able to differentiate yourself from others, become an expert in your field, and attract the right clients. This will help you build a successful consulting business that provides value to your clients and generates income for you.

In conclusion, defining your niche is an important step in the process of starting your own consulting business. By taking the time to assess your skills and interests, research the market, identify your ideal client, evaluate your competition, and test your niche, you'll be well on your way to success.

Chapter 3

Conducting Market Research

Before you start your consulting business, it's important to conduct thorough market research. Market research will help you understand your target market, identify potential clients, and determine the demand for your services.

Why Conduct Market Research?

Conducting market research is an important step in the process of starting your own consulting business. There are several reasons why it's important to conduct market research, including:

- Understanding Your Target Market: Market research will help you understand the needs and preferences of your target market. This information will be critical in developing your services, pricing your services, and creating a marketing strategy that resonates with your target market.

- Identifying Potential Clients: Market research will help you identify potential clients and target your marketing efforts. You'll be able to see who is in need of your services and what type of businesses are most likely to hire a consultant.

- Determining Demand for Your Services: Market research will help you determine the demand for your services. This information will help you decide if there is a market for your services and if your consulting business is viable.

How to Conduct Market Research

Conducting market research can seem daunting, but it doesn't have to be. Here are some steps you can take to conduct effective market research:

1. Determine Your Target Market: Before you start your market research, it's important to determine your target market. Who are you trying to reach with your services? What are their needs and preferences?

2. Gather Secondary Data: Secondary data is information that has already been collected by others. This includes data from government sources, trade associations, and market research firms. Secondary data can provide a wealth of information about your target market and help you understand the demand for your services.

3. Conduct Surveys: Surveys can be a great way to gather information about your target market. You can conduct surveys online, in person, or over the phone. Surveys can help you understand the needs and preferences of your target market and determine the demand for your services.

4. Conduct Focus Groups: Focus groups are a great way to gather qualitative data about your target market. Focus groups consist of a small group of people who are asked to provide feedback on your services, pricing, and marketing efforts.

5. Analyze Your Competitors: Take a look at your competition to see what they're offering and what they're not offering. This information can help you understand the market and determine the demand for your services.

Once you've completed your market research, you'll have a better understanding of your target market and the demand for your services. This information will be critical in developing your services, pricing your services, and creating a marketing strategy that resonates with your target market.

The Importance of Staying Focused

Conducting market research is a time-consuming process, but it's essential to the success of your consulting business. By taking the time to understand your target market and determine the demand for your services, you'll be better equipped to make informed decisions about your services, pricing, and marketing efforts.

It's also important to stay focused during the market research process. Don't try to gather too much information at once, as this can be overwhelming and lead to information overload. Instead, focus on gathering the information that's most critical to your consulting business and use that information to make informed decisions.

In conclusion, conducting market research is an important step in the process of starting your own consulting business. By taking the time to understand your target market and determine the demand for your services, you'll be better equipped to make informed decisions and build a successful consulting business

Chapter 4

Creating a Business Plan

A business plan is a critical tool for the success of your consulting business. It outlines your goals, strategies, and the steps you'll take to achieve success. A well-written business plan will serve as a roadmap for your business, help you secure funding, and provide a clear plan of action.

Why You Need a Business Plan

A business plan is essential to the success of your consulting business for several reasons, including:

- It Helps You Stay Focused: A business plan will help you stay focused on your goals and the steps you need to take to achieve success. It will serve as a roadmap for your business, helping you stay on track and avoid getting sidetracked by unimportant tasks.

- It Helps You Secure Funding: If you're looking to secure funding from investors or lenders, a business plan is a must. Investors and lenders will want to see a well-written plan that outlines your goals and strategies, as well as your financial projections.

- It Provides a Clear Plan of Action: A business plan will provide a clear plan of action for your business. It will outline the steps you'll take to achieve success, including marketing, sales, and customer service.

What to Include in Your Business Plan

A business plan should include several key elements, including:

- Executive Summary: This section provides a brief overview of your business and includes your goals, strategies, and financial projections.

- Company Description: This section provides a detailed description of your business, including your mission statement, business structure, and services.

- Market Analysis: This section includes your market research and provides a detailed analysis of your target market and the demand for your services.

- Competitive Analysis: This section includes a detailed analysis of your competition, including their strengths and weaknesses.

- Sales and Marketing Strategies: This section includes your sales and marketing strategies, including your unique value proposition, target market, and marketing budget.

- Financial Projections: This section includes your financial projections, including your projected income and expenses.

- Action Plan: This section includes a step-by-step plan of action for your business, including milestones and deadlines.

How to Write a Business Plan

Writing a business plan can seem daunting, but it doesn't have to be. Here are some tips to help you get started:

1. Start with a Outline: Start by creating an outline of your business plan. This will help you stay organized and ensure that you cover all the important elements.

2. Do Your Research: Before you start writing your business plan, be sure to conduct thorough market research and analyze your competition. This information will be critical in developing your business plan.

3. Be Realistic: When writing your financial projections, be realistic. Don't overstate your projections or make unrealistic assumptions. Be sure to include a worst-case scenario and a best-case scenario to help you prepare for any eventualities.

4. Seek Feedback: Once you've written your business plan, seek feedback from others. Ask friends, family members, and business associates for their opinions and suggestions.

5. Update Your Plan: As your business grows and changes, be sure to update your business plan. Your plan should evolve with your business and reflect your current goals and strategies.

In conclusion, a business plan is an essential tool for the success of your consulting business. It outlines your goals, strategies, and the steps you'll take to achieve success, and serves as a roadmap for your business. By taking the time to create a well-written business plan, you'll be better equipped to secure funding, stay focused,

Chapter 5

Registering Your Business

Congratulations, you're one step closer to starting your own consulting business! The next step is to register your business, which is a crucial step in establishing your business as a legitimate entity. This process will vary depending on where you live and the type of business you plan to start, but in this chapter, we'll cover the basics of registering your business.

Why You Need to Register Your Business

There are several reasons why you need to register your business, including:

- Legal Protection: Registering your business will give you legal protection and help you avoid personal liability for the debts and obligations of your business.

- Establishing Your Brand: Registering your business will give you the ability to establish your brand and protect your business name.

- Tax Benefits: Registering your business can also provide tax benefits, including the ability to deduct business expenses and access to tax credits.

Types of Business Structures

Before you register your business, you'll need to decide on the type of business structure you want to use. The most common types of business structures include:

- Sole Proprietorship: A sole proprietorship is the simplest type of business structure, and is typically used by individuals who own and operate their business. In this structure, the owner is personally responsible for all debts and obligations of the business.

- Partnership: A partnership is a business structure that involves two or more individuals who own and operate the business together. In this structure, each partner is personally responsible for the debts and obligations of the business.

- Limited Liability Company (LLC): An LLC is a business structure that provides the personal liability protection of a corporation while retaining the tax benefits of a partnership. In this structure, the owners are known as members, and they are not personally responsible for the debts and obligations of the business.

- Corporation: A corporation is a separate legal entity from its owners, and is typically used by larger businesses. In this structure, the owners are known as shareholders, and they are not personally responsible for the debts and obligations of the business.

Choosing the Right Business Structure

Choosing the right business structure for your consulting business can be a challenging decision. You'll want to consider several factors, including your personal liability, tax implications, and the level of control you want to have over your business.

To help you make an informed decision, it's a good idea to speak with a legal professional or an accountant. They can provide you with guidance and help you choose the business structure that's right for your consulting business.

Registering Your Business

Once you've decided on the type of business structure you want to use, it's time to register your business. The process will vary depending on where you live and the type of business you plan to start, but typically, you'll need to:

- Choose a Business Name: Choose a business name that's unique and memorable, and check to see if it's available in your state. You may also need to register your business name with your state.

- Obtain any Required Licenses and Permits: Depending on your business, you may need to obtain specific licenses and permits. This can include a business license, a sales tax permit, or a professional license.

- Register with Your State: Register your business with your state, which typically involves filing articles of incorporation or a certificate of formation.

- Obtain an EIN: Obtain an Employer Identification Number (EIN) from the Internal Revenue Service (IRS), which is used to identify your business for tax purposes.

Register for Taxes: Register your business for taxes, including business income tax, sales tax, and any other taxes that may apply to your business. You'll also need to determine if you need to collect sales tax on the services you provide and if so, register with your state's tax authority.

- Get Business Insurance: It's a good idea to get business insurance to protect your business from potential risks. This can include liability insurance, which protects your business from claims made by customers or clients, and property insurance, which protects your business from damage to its physical assets.

- Set Up a Business Bank Account: Setting up a separate business bank account will help you keep your personal and business finances separate, which makes it easier to manage your business finances and track expenses.

- Create a Business Plan: Finally, create a detailed business plan that outlines your business goals, strategies, and plans for growth. Your business plan should also include a financial plan, which includes your expected income and expenses, and a marketing plan, which outlines how you plan to promote your consulting business.

Conclusion

Registering your business is an important step in starting your own consulting business. By following these steps and seeking the advice of a legal professional or an accountant, you'll be well on your way to establishing your business as a legitimate entity and setting yourself up for success. Remember, this is just the beginning of your journey as a consultant, and with hard work, dedication, and a passion for helping others, you'll be able to achieve your goals and succeed in your business.

Chapter 6.

Building a Strong Brand

In the world of consulting, your brand is your reputation. It's what sets you apart from your competition and helps you establish credibility and trust with your potential clients. A strong brand can make all the difference when it comes to attracting and retaining clients, so it's important to put thought and effort into building a brand that represents your business in the best light. In this chapter, we'll discuss the key elements of building a strong brand for your consulting business.

Define Your Brand Identity

The first step in building a strong brand is to define your brand identity. This includes your mission statement, values, and what sets you apart from your competition. Think about what you stand for and what you want to communicate to your clients. Are you passionate about helping businesses save time and money? Do you specialize in a specific industry? What sets you apart from other consultants? Once you have a clear understanding of your brand identity, you can start to build a brand that accurately reflects who you are and what you do.

Develop a Visual Identity

Your visual identity is an essential component of your brand. This includes your logo, color scheme, typography, and other design elements that will be used across all of your marketing materials. When developing your visual identity, it's important to keep your brand identity in mind and choose design elements that accurately reflect who you are and what you do. Make sure your visual identity is simple, memorable, and consistent across all of your materials.

Establish a Strong Online Presence

In today's digital age, it's essential to have a strong online presence. This includes a professional website, social media profiles, and online directories. Your website should be easy to navigate, visually appealing, and include information about your business, services, and contact information. Your social media profiles should be active and regularly updated, and you should consider listing your business in online directories to increase visibility and help potential clients find you.

Use Consistent Messaging

Consistent messaging is key to building a strong brand. Make sure all of your marketing materials, including your website, business cards, and social media profiles, use the same tone of voice, messaging, and design elements. This will help you build a cohesive brand image and increase recognition and trust with your potential clients.

Incorporate Storytelling

People remember stories, so incorporating storytelling into your branding can be a powerful way to build a connection with your potential clients. Think about your journey as a consultant and the unique challenges and successes you've experienced. Share these stories in your marketing materials to humanize your brand and help potential clients see the value of your services.

Build Relationships with Your Clients

Finally, building strong relationships with your clients is an essential part of building a strong brand. Make sure you communicate regularly with your clients, respond to their needs and concerns, and provide high-quality services that exceed their expectations. By building strong relationships with your clients, you'll not only establish trust and credibility, but you'll also increase the chances of retaining clients and getting referrals.

Conclusion

Building a strong brand is essential for the success of your consulting business. By defining your brand identity, developing a visual identity, establishing a strong online presence, using consistent messaging, incorporating storytelling, and building relationships with your clients, you'll be able to create a brand that accurately reflects who you are and what you do, and sets you apart from your competition. Remember, building a strong brand takes time and effort, but the payoff is worth it in the long run.

Chapter 7

Setting Up Your Office

As a consultant, your office is your headquarters, where you'll be conducting your business, meeting with clients, and conducting research. It's important to create an environment that is professional, comfortable, and conducive to productivity. In this chapter, we'll discuss the key elements of setting up your office and how to create an environment that supports your success.

Choosing Your Office Location

The first step in setting up your office is choosing the right location. Consider factors such as accessibility, cost, and proximity to clients and potential clients. If you'll be meeting with clients frequently, it's important to choose a location that is easily accessible by car or public transportation. If cost is a concern, consider working from home or renting a shared office space.

Furnishing Your Office

Once you've chosen your office location, it's time to furnish it. Make sure you have a comfortable chair, desk, and lighting that supports productivity. Invest in a high-quality printer and scanner, and consider purchasing a laptop or desktop computer to help you stay connected and productive on the go. Don't forget to decorate your office with personal touches, such as photos, plants, and artwork, to create a warm and welcoming environment.

Organizing Your Office

Organization is key to productivity, so it's important to keep your office tidy and organized. Make sure you have a system in place for filing important documents and consider purchasing a desk organizer to keep your desk clutter-free. If you'll be storing client information, make sure you have a secure filing cabinet to keep it confidential and protected.

Setting Up a Communication System

Having a reliable communication system is essential for any business, and your consulting business is no exception. Consider purchasing a business phone line and a fax machine to keep in touch with clients, and make sure you have a reliable email system in place to communicate with clients and colleagues. Consider investing in a virtual phone system that allows you to forward calls to your cell phone when you're away from your office.

Creating a Comfortable Workspace

Creating a comfortable workspace is essential for productivity and well-being. Make sure your office is well-lit, temperature-controlled, and free of distractions. Consider adding plants, artwork, or photos to create a warm and welcoming environment. Invest in a good ergonomic chair to support your posture and comfort, and make sure you take regular breaks to stretch and move around.

Conclusion

Setting up a professional and comfortable office is essential for the success of your consulting business. By choosing the right location, furnishing your office with essential equipment and personal touches, organizing your office, setting up a communication system, and creating a comfortable workspace, you'll be able to create an environment that supports your success and well-being. Remember, your office is your headquarters, and it's important to create an environment that is professional, productive, and supportive of your success.

Chapter 8.

Networking and Marketing

Networking and marketing are two of the most important elements of starting and growing a successful consulting business. In this chapter, we'll discuss the key elements of networking and marketing and how to build a strong network of contacts and promote your business effectively.

Networking

Networking is the process of building relationships and connecting with others in your industry. This can include attending industry events, participating in professional organizations, and reaching out to potential clients and referral partners. Building a strong network of contacts is essential for finding new clients, building relationships with potential referral partners, and staying informed about industry trends and developments.

To be successful at networking, it's important to be prepared and to have a clear understanding of what you bring to the table. Make sure you have a clear and concise elevator pitch that highlights your skills, experience, and the benefits you bring to your clients. Dress professionally, bring business cards, and be prepared to engage in meaningful conversations.

Marketing

Marketing is the process of promoting your business and reaching potential clients. There are many different marketing strategies you can use to reach your target market, including online advertising, social media marketing, email marketing, and direct mail. When developing your marketing plan, it's important to consider your target market, your budget, and your goals.

Online Advertising

Online advertising is a cost-effective way to reach a large audience. Consider advertising on websites and social media platforms that are popular with your target market. You can also use targeted advertising to reach specific groups of people based on their interests, location, and other factors.

Social Media Marketing

Social media is a powerful tool for promoting your business and connecting with potential clients. Consider creating a business page on popular platforms such as LinkedIn, Twitter, and Facebook, and use these platforms to share industry news, updates on your business, and information about your services. Make sure you engage with your followers and respond to their questions and comments in a timely and professional manner.

Email Marketing

Email marketing is a cost-effective way to reach potential clients and build relationships. Consider creating a newsletter or e-mail campaign that highlights your services and the benefits you bring to your clients. Make sure your emails are professional, well-written, and optimized for open and click-through rates.

Direct Mail

Direct mail is a physical marketing method that involves sending promotional materials, such as brochures or flyers, directly to potential clients. This can be an effective way to reach a targeted audience and build relationships with potential clients. Consider including a special offer or discount to encourage potential clients to take action.

Conclusion

Networking and marketing are essential elements of starting and growing a successful consulting business. By building a strong network of contacts, promoting your business effectively, and reaching potential clients through a variety of marketing strategies, you'll be able to grow your business and achieve your goals. Remember, networking and marketing take time, effort, and persistence, so be patient, stay focused, and keep working at it.

Chapter 9

Establishing Your Rates and Packages

As a consultant, one of the most important decisions you'll make is determining your rates and packages. This can be a challenging process, as you want to charge enough to make a profit and provide value to your clients, while also being competitive and appealing to potential clients. In this chapter, we'll discuss the key elements of establishing your rates and packages, including determining your costs, researching your competition, and developing appealing packages for your clients.

Determining Your Costs

The first step in establishing your rates is to determine your costs. This includes your business expenses, such as rent, utilities, and equipment, as well as your personal expenses, such as food, housing, and transportation. You'll also need to factor in your desired profit margin, which will help you determine your minimum hourly rate or package price.

To determine your costs, start by creating a budget for your business. Make sure you include all of your fixed and variable expenses, such as rent, utilities, equipment, marketing and advertising, and any other costs associated with running your business. Once you have a clear understanding of your costs, you can calculate your desired profit margin and determine your minimum hourly rate or package price.

Researching Your Competition

Once you have determined your costs, you'll want to research your competition to see what they are charging for similar services. This will help you determine if your rates are in line with the market and if you need to adjust them to be more competitive. When researching your competition, make sure you look at a variety of factors, including their experience, skills, and the value they bring to their clients.

Developing Packages

In addition to setting hourly rates, you can also develop packages for your clients. Packages can include a set number of hours, specific services, and a set price. Packages can be a great way to appeal to potential clients and provide them with a clear understanding of what they'll receive for their investment. When developing your packages, make sure you consider the needs and budget of your target market, as well as the value you bring to your clients.

Pricing Strategies

There are several pricing strategies you can use when setting your rates and developing your packages, including value-based pricing, premium pricing, and loss leader pricing.

Value-based pricing is when you charge based on the value you bring to your clients, rather than the time you spend working. This can be a great way to appeal to high-end clients and establish yourself as an expert in your field.

Premium pricing is when you charge a higher rate than your competition for similar services. This can be a great way to appeal to clients who value quality and expertise, and are willing to pay a premium for it.

Loss leader pricing is when you offer a low-priced package or service to attract new clients, with the expectation that they'll invest in more expensive services in the future. This can be a great way to build relationships with new clients and generate future business.

Conclusion

Establishing your rates and packages is a critical step in starting and growing your consulting business. By determining your costs, researching your competition, and developing appealing packages for your clients, you'll be able to charge competitive rates, provide value to your clients, and make a profit. Remember, it's important to be flexible and willing to adjust your rates and packages as needed, as the market and your business evolves.

Chapter 10.

Hiring and Managing Staff

As your consulting business grows, you may reach a point where you need to hire staff to support your business. Hiring and managing employees can be both exciting and challenging, and it's important to have a solid plan in place to ensure success. In this chapter, we'll discuss the key elements of hiring and managing staff, including recruiting and hiring, training and development, and performance management.

Recruiting and Hiring

The first step in hiring staff is to determine your staffing needs and the skills and experience required for each position. This will help you identify the type of employees you need to hire and the best places to find them. You can find potential employees through job postings, referrals from friends and colleagues, and professional networking sites.

Once you have identified potential candidates, it's important to conduct thorough interviews and reference checks to ensure you are hiring the right person for the job. During the interview process, be sure to ask questions that are relevant to the position and evaluate the candidate's skills, experience, and personality to determine if they would be a good fit for your business.

Training and Development

Once you have hired your staff, it's important to provide them with the training and development they need to be successful in their roles. This can include on-the-job training, workshops, and training sessions, as well as access to online resources and materials. Providing your employees with the training and development they need will help them grow and develop as professionals, and will contribute to the success of your business.

Performance Management

Performance management is the process of monitoring and evaluating employee performance to ensure they are meeting expectations and contributing to the success of your business. This includes setting performance goals, providing regular feedback and coaching, and conducting performance evaluations. Performance management is an ongoing process and should be integrated into your daily operations and routines.

Managing Employee Relations

In addition to performance management, it's important to have a plan in place for managing employee relations. This includes establishing clear policies and procedures for communication, addressing employee concerns and complaints, and handling disciplinary issues and conflict resolution. By having a plan in place for managing employee relations, you can ensure that your employees feel supported and valued, and that your business runs smoothly.

Conclusion

Hiring and managing staff can be a rewarding experience, but it requires careful planning and preparation. By determining your staffing needs, conducting thorough interviews and reference checks, providing training and development, and managing employee relations, you'll be able to build a strong and effective team that supports the success of your business. Remember, investing in your employees and fostering a positive work environment will pay dividends in the long-run, so don't be afraid to put in the time and effort required to build a great team.

Chapter 11.

Financial Planning and Budgeting

As a consulting business owner, financial planning and budgeting is an essential aspect of your success. Your finances will determine your ability to grow and sustain your business, and it's important to have a solid plan in place to ensure you are managing your finances effectively. In this chapter, we'll discuss the key elements of financial planning and budgeting, including setting financial goals, creating a budget, managing cash flow, and tracking your finances.

Setting Financial Goals

Before you can begin planning and budgeting your finances, you need to establish your financial goals. This will help you determine how much money you need to earn and how much you need to save to reach your goals. Your financial goals may include paying off debt, saving for retirement, or investing in your business. Once you have established your financial goals, you can begin to plan and budget your finances accordingly.

Creating a Budget

A budget is a tool that helps you manage your finances by tracking your income and expenses and ensuring that you are spending money wisely. Your budget should include all of your fixed expenses, such as rent, utilities, and insurance, as well as your variable expenses, such as marketing and advertising. By creating a budget, you can see where your money is going, identify areas where you can save money, and track your progress towards your financial goals.

Managing Cash Flow

Cash flow is the amount of money coming in and going out of your business. It's important to manage your cash flow effectively to ensure that you have enough money to meet your financial obligations and reach your goals. There are several strategies you can use to manage your cash flow, such as invoicing clients promptly, collecting payments on time, and reducing your expenses.

Tracking Your Finances

To ensure that you are managing your finances effectively, it's important to track your income and expenses regularly. You can use software, such as QuickBooks or Xero, or a simple spreadsheet to track your finances. By tracking your finances regularly, you can see how your business is performing, identify areas where you can improve, and make informed decisions about how to grow and sustain your business.

Conclusion

Financial planning and budgeting is an essential aspect of your success as a consulting business owner. By setting financial goals, creating a budget, managing cash flow, and tracking your finances, you can ensure that you are managing your finances effectively and growing your business. Remember, taking control of your finances is the key to reaching your goals, so be sure to invest the time and effort required to build a solid financial plan.

Chapter 12.

Securing Funding

Starting a consulting business can be expensive, and you may need to secure funding to cover the costs of setting up your business and growing it. There are several options available to you, including loans, grants, and investments. In this chapter, we'll discuss the key elements of securing funding, including preparing a funding proposal, finding the right funding sources, and understanding the terms and conditions of loans and investments.

Preparing a Funding Proposal

Before you can secure funding, you need to prepare a funding proposal. A funding proposal is a document that outlines your business idea, its potential for success, and the amount of funding you need to achieve your goals. Your funding proposal should include an executive summary, a detailed business plan, financial projections, and information about your management team.

Finding the Right Funding Sources

There are many different funding sources available to you, including banks, credit unions, angel investors, and venture capitalists. Each funding source has its own criteria for funding, and you need to find the right funding source to meet your needs. For example, if you have a strong business idea and a solid business plan, you may be able to secure funding from an angel investor or venture capitalist. However, if you have a less developed business idea, you may need to start with a loan from a bank or credit union.

Understanding the Terms and Conditions of Loans and Investments

When you secure funding, you will be required to repay the loan or return the investment, plus interest or other charges. It's important to understand the terms and conditions of the loan or investment, including the repayment schedule, interest rate, and other fees. By understanding the terms and conditions of the loan or investment, you can make an informed decision about whether the funding is right for you and your business.

Securing Funding from the Government

There are several government programs available to help small businesses secure funding, including the Small Business Administration (SBA) and the Minority Business Development Agency (MBDA). These programs provide loans, grants, and other forms of funding to help businesses start and grow. To apply for government funding, you will need to submit a funding proposal and meet the criteria set by the government.

Conclusion

Securing funding is an important step in starting and growing your consulting business. By preparing a funding proposal, finding the right funding sources, and understanding the terms and conditions of loans and investments, you can ensure that you have the resources you need to succeed. Remember, securing funding is just one aspect of starting and growing your business, and you need to focus on building a strong business plan, creating a strong brand, and delivering excellent service to your clients.

Chapter 13

Understanding Legal Issues

Starting a consulting business involves a number of legal considerations, and it's important to understand the laws and regulations that apply to your business. In this chapter, we'll discuss some of the key legal issues you need to consider when starting your own consulting business, including registering your business, obtaining necessary licenses and permits, and protecting your intellectual property.

Registering Your Business

Before you can start your consulting business, you need to register it with the appropriate government agencies. This typically involves choosing a business structure, such as a sole proprietorship, partnership, limited liability company (LLC), or corporation, and registering your business with the Secretary of State. You may also need to register for a tax ID number and obtain any necessary licenses or permits.

Obtaining Licenses and Permits

Depending on the type of consulting services you provide, you may need to obtain certain licenses and permits. For example, if you provide consulting services in a regulated industry, such as health care or finance, you may need to obtain a professional license. You should research the requirements for your specific business and obtain any necessary licenses and permits before you start operating.

Protecting Your Intellectual Property

As a consultant, you may create or use a variety of intellectual property, including trademarks, copyrights, and trade secrets. It's important to understand the laws that protect these assets and to take steps to protect your intellectual property. For example, you may want to register trademarks for your business name and logo, and to use copyrights to protect your original works, such as articles, presentations, and reports.

Managing Contracts and Agreements

As a consultant, you will likely enter into contracts and agreements with clients, vendors, and employees. It's important to understand the terms of these agreements and to ensure that they are legally binding. You may want to work with an attorney to draft contracts and agreements and to review any contracts or agreements that you enter into.

Insurance and Liability Issues

Consulting businesses are exposed to a variety of risks, and it's important to protect your business from these risks by obtaining insurance coverage. For example, you may need to obtain general liability insurance, professional liability insurance, and business interruption insurance. You should work with an insurance agent to determine the types of insurance coverage that are appropriate for your business and to obtain quotes from insurance companies.

Conclusion

Understanding legal issues is an important part of starting and operating a successful consulting business. By registering your business, obtaining necessary licenses and permits, protecting your intellectual property, managing contracts and agreements, and obtaining insurance coverage, you can ensure that your business is compliant with the law and protected from risks. Remember, the laws and regulations that apply to your business can change over time, and it's important to stay informed and to work with an attorney if you have any questions or concerns.

Chapter 14

Building a Strong Network of Partners

Networking is an essential part of building a successful consulting business. By building a strong network of partners, you can expand your reach, increase your exposure, and find new clients. In this chapter, we'll discuss some of the key strategies for building a strong network of partners, including attending industry events, collaborating with other businesses, and leveraging social media.

Attending Industry Events

Attending industry events is a great way to meet new people and build relationships with potential partners. Whether you attend conferences, trade shows, or networking events, these events provide an opportunity to connect with others in your industry and to learn about the latest trends and developments. When you attend industry events, be sure to bring business cards and to be prepared to network.

Collaborating with Other Businesses

Collaborating with other businesses can be a great way to expand your reach and build relationships with potential partners. For example, you could partner with another consulting firm to offer joint services, or you could work with a complementary business, such as a marketing firm or a software company, to offer bundled services to your clients. When you collaborate with other businesses, be sure to carefully consider the terms of the partnership and to clearly define each party's responsibilities and expectations.

Leveraging Social Media

Social media can be a powerful tool for building a strong network of partners. By using platforms such as LinkedIn, Twitter, and Facebook, you can connect with others in your industry, share your expertise, and build relationships with potential partners. When you use social media, be sure to engage with others, share valuable content, and participate in online communities related to your industry.

Building Relationships

Building relationships with potential partners takes time and effort, but it can pay off in the long run. When you meet potential partners, be sure to listen more than you talk, and to focus on building trust and rapport. Offer to help others whenever you can, and be willing to invest time and energy in building relationships. Over time, these relationships can lead to opportunities for collaboration and business growth.

Conclusion

Building a strong network of partners is essential for growing your consulting business. By attending industry events, collaborating with other businesses, leveraging social media, and building relationships, you can expand your reach, increase your exposure, and find new clients. Remember, building a strong network of partners takes time and effort, but it can pay off in the long run. So be patient, be persistent, and be willing to invest in your network.

Chapter 15

Utilizing Technology and Tools

In today's digital age, technology and tools play a crucial role in the success of a consulting business. From project management software to virtual meeting platforms, the right technology and tools can help you work more efficiently, communicate more effectively, and deliver better results for your clients. In this chapter, we'll discuss some of the key technology and tools you should consider for your consulting business, and how to make the most of them.

Project Management Software

Project management software is a must-have for any consulting business. With this type of software, you can easily keep track of projects, deadlines, and team members, and ensure that everything runs smoothly. Popular options include Asana, Trello, and Basecamp, each with their own set of features and pricing options. When choosing project management software, be sure to consider your specific needs and the size of your team.

Virtual Meeting Platforms

Virtual meeting platforms are essential for consulting businesses that work with clients remotely. With platforms like Zoom, Skype, and Google Meet, you can conduct virtual meetings, give presentations, and collaborate with clients and team members from anywhere in the world. When choosing a virtual meeting platform, be sure to consider the features you need, such as screen sharing, recording, and virtual backgrounds, and to test the platform before using it for important meetings.

Communication Tools

Effective communication is crucial for any consulting business, and the right communication tools can help. Whether you prefer email, instant messaging, or project management software, choose tools that work for you and your team, and that allow you to communicate effectively and efficiently. When using communication tools, be sure to establish clear guidelines and protocols, and to keep your team informed of any updates or changes.

Time Tracking and Invoicing Tools

Time tracking and invoicing tools are important for keeping your business organized and for getting paid for your work. With these tools, you can easily track your time and expenses, generate invoices, and manage your cash flow. Popular options include FreshBooks, QuickBooks, and Toggl. When choosing time tracking and invoicing tools, be sure to consider your specific needs and to look for tools that integrate with other software you use.

Conclusion

The right technology and tools can help you run your consulting business more efficiently, communicate more effectively, and deliver better results for your clients. From project management software to virtual meeting platforms, be sure to choose tools that work for you and your team, and that allow you to get the job done. And don't be afraid to experiment and try new tools. By staying up-to-date on the latest technology and tools, you can continue to grow your consulting business and stay ahead of the curve.

Chapter 16

Staying Up-to-Date with Industry Trends

Starting your own consulting business can be an exciting journey, but it is also important to stay current with industry trends to remain competitive and relevant in the market. The consulting field is constantly evolving and adapting, and staying informed on the latest developments can help you stay ahead of the game. Here are a few tips on how to stay up-to-date with industry trends.

1. Read industry publications: One of the simplest ways to stay informed is to read industry publications. There are many trade magazines and websites that focus on the consulting industry and provide the latest news, insights, and trends. Some popular publications include Consulting magazine, Strategy + Business, and the Harvard Business Review. These publications provide valuable insights into the latest consulting techniques, best practices, and market trends, and can help you stay ahead of the curve.

2. Attend conferences and events: Attending conferences and events can be a great way to stay current with industry trends. These events bring together experts and professionals from the consulting industry, and provide a platform for sharing ideas and best practices. Some popular consulting events include the International Management Consulting Conference, the Annual European Management Conference, and the World Business Forum. These events can be an excellent opportunity to network with industry professionals,

learn from thought leaders, and stay up-to-date with the latest industry trends.

3. Follow thought leaders: Following thought leaders in the consulting industry can provide valuable insights into industry trends. Thought leaders are individuals who have made a significant impact in the field, and they often share their insights and opinions through social media, blogs, and other channels. You can follow consultants, authors, and influencers in the consulting field to stay informed on the latest developments in the industry.

4. Participate in professional organizations: Joining professional organizations can be a great way to stay up-to-date with industry trends. Professional organizations provide a platform for sharing information, knowledge, and best practices, and they often host events and webinars to educate members on the latest developments in the field. Some popular consulting organizations include the Institute of Management, the Association of Management Consulting Firms, and the International Association of Business Consultants.

5. Stay connected with your clients: Your clients can also be a valuable source of information on industry trends. Staying connected with your clients and understanding their needs and challenges can provide insights into the latest developments in the consulting industry. This can help you stay ahead of the curve and develop new services and offerings that meet your clients' needs.

In conclusion, staying up-to-date with industry trends is essential for success in the consulting business. Whether you choose to read industry publications, attend conferences and events, follow thought leaders, participate in professional organizations, or stay connected with your clients, taking the time to stay informed can provide valuable insights and help you remain competitive in the market.

Chapter 17

Providing Excellent Customer Service

As a consultant, your main goal is to provide your clients with the best possible service and help them achieve their goals. To do this, you must have a deep understanding of your clients' needs and provide them with the right solutions and support. One of the most important aspects of providing excellent customer service is being responsive, helpful and professional at all times.

Responsiveness

Responsiveness is key when it comes to providing customer service. Your clients want to know that you are available to help them when they need it, and that you will be there for them when things go wrong. You can demonstrate your responsiveness by answering your phone or responding to emails within a reasonable time frame. Make sure you also have a system in place for following up with clients, so that you can keep track of their needs and progress.

Helpfulness

In order to provide excellent customer service, you need to be helpful. This means being able to answer questions and solve problems quickly and efficiently. You should also be proactive in suggesting solutions that will help your clients achieve their goals. This will not only help you build trust with your clients, but it will also help you to establish yourself as an expert in your field.

Professionalism

Professionalism is also key when it comes to providing excellent customer service. You should always be professional and courteous, even when dealing with difficult clients. You should also be knowledgeable about your industry and be able to provide your clients with accurate and up-to-date information. This will help you build a strong reputation as a reliable and trustworthy consultant.

Customer Feedback

One of the best ways to improve your customer service is to ask for feedback from your clients. This can be done through surveys, one-on-one meetings, or by simply asking them how you can better serve them. Be open to criticism and use this feedback to make improvements in your service. This will not only help you to provide better customer service, but it will also help you to build a loyal and satisfied customer base.

Conclusion

Providing excellent customer service is essential to the success of your consulting business. By being responsive, helpful, and professional, you can establish yourself as an expert in your field and build a strong reputation as a reliable and trustworthy consultant. Don't forget to ask for feedback and use it to improve your service, as this will help you to build a loyal and satisfied customer base. Remember, happy customers are the key to the success of your business.

Chapter 18.

Measuring Your Success

Congratulations! You've taken the leap and started your own consulting business. You've put in a lot of hard work to get here and it's important to take a step back and reflect on your progress. Measuring your success is a critical part of any business and will help you identify areas for improvement, celebrate your achievements and keep you motivated.

Defining Success

The first step in measuring your success is to define what success means to you. This is personal and unique to your business and may include goals such as financial stability, customer satisfaction, employee happiness, or personal satisfaction. Write down your definition of success and keep it in a place where you can see it every day to keep you motivated.

Setting Key Performance Indicators (KPIs)

Once you've defined success, it's time to set key performance indicators (KPIs) that will help you track your progress towards your goals. KPIs are specific, measurable, and time-bound targets that allow you to track your progress over time. Common KPIs for consulting businesses include revenue, customer satisfaction, employee satisfaction, and new client acquisition.

Tracking Progress

Now that you have your KPIs, it's time to start tracking your progress. There are a variety of tools and technologies available to help you track your KPIs, including spreadsheets, business intelligence software, and customer relationship management (CRM) systems. Choose the tools that work best for you and your business and set up a regular process for tracking your KPIs.

Evaluating Results

Once you have tracked your KPIs for a period of time, it's time to evaluate your results. This is the time to ask yourself whether you are making progress towards your goals and what changes you need to make to improve. Analyze your results, identify areas for improvement and set new goals for the next period.

Celebrating Your Successes

Finally, don't forget to celebrate your successes! This is a critical part of measuring your success and will help you stay motivated and focused on your goals. Whether it's treating yourself to a night out, taking a day off, or just taking a moment to appreciate your achievements, celebrating your successes is an important part of staying motivated and driven.

In conclusion, measuring your success is an important part of running a successful consulting business. By defining your definition of success, setting KPIs, tracking your progress, evaluating results and celebrating your successes, you can keep yourself motivated and focused on your goals. So, take the time to measure your success and enjoy the journey!

Chapter 19

Continuously Improving Your Services

As a consultant, it's important to always strive for excellence and continuously improve the services you offer to your clients. Your clients will appreciate the extra effort you put into ensuring that they receive the best possible service, and it can also help you stand out from your competitors. Here are some tips for continuously improving your services as a consultant.

1. Ask for feedback: One of the best ways to improve your services is to ask your clients for feedback. You can ask them directly after a project is completed, or you can send out a survey to get a more comprehensive understanding of their thoughts and experiences. Use the feedback to identify areas where you can make improvements, and don't be afraid to ask follow-up questions to gain more insight.

2. Stay current with industry trends: Keeping up-to-date with the latest industry trends is crucial for continuous improvement. This will allow you to stay ahead of the curve and ensure that your services are cutting-edge and relevant to your clients' needs. Attend conferences and workshops, read trade publications, and network with other consultants to stay informed about the latest developments in your field.

3. Invest in professional development: Investing in your own professional development is key to continuous improvement. Attend workshops, conferences, and training sessions to gain new skills and knowledge, and

take advantage of online resources such as webinars, e-books, and online courses.

4. Collaborate with other consultants: Collaborating with other consultants can be a great way to exchange ideas and learn from each other. Join a professional association or attend networking events to meet other consultants in your field. You can also join online forums or discussion groups where you can engage with other consultants and exchange ideas and best practices.

5. Stay organized: Staying organized can help you be more efficient and effective in delivering your services. Use project management tools and software to help you keep track of tasks, deadlines, and client communication. You can also use calendars, schedules, and to-do lists to help you stay on top of your responsibilities and ensure that you're providing the best possible service to your clients.

6. Review your services regularly: Regularly review your services to identify areas for improvement. This can help you identify any gaps in your offerings, and make changes to ensure that you're providing the best possible service to your clients. Ask your clients for feedback, and use that feedback to make improvements to your services.

In conclusion, continuously improving your services is crucial for success as a consultant. By asking for feedback, staying current with industry trends, investing in professional development, collaborating with other consultants, staying organized, and regularly reviewing your services, you can ensure that you're always providing the best possible service to your clients.

Chapter 20

Maintaining a Healthy Work-Life Balance

Starting and running your own consulting business can be a rewarding and fulfilling experience, but it can also be demanding and time-consuming. It's essential to maintain a healthy work-life balance in order to avoid burnout and ensure that you are able to continue providing the best services to your clients. In this chapter, we will explore ways to maintain a healthy balance between work and life.

First and foremost, it's important to set clear boundaries between your work life and personal life. This can include setting specific times for work and times for rest, as well as separating your work and personal space. For example, if you work from home, it can be helpful to have a dedicated workspace that you only use for work. This helps to create a mental and physical separation between work and life.

Next, it's important to prioritize self-care. This can include making time for exercise, getting enough sleep, eating a balanced diet, and engaging in hobbies or other activities that you enjoy. Taking care of your mental and physical health will help you to be more productive and effective in your work, and it will also improve your overall quality of life.

Another important aspect of maintaining a healthy work-life balance is delegating responsibilities and delegating tasks to others when possible. This can include hiring employees, outsourcing tasks, or partnering with other businesses. By delegating tasks, you can free up time to focus on the most important aspects of your business, such as developing new services, networking, and growing your business.

Finally, it's important to be mindful of the impact that your work has on your family and friends. This may involve setting clear boundaries with them as well, and making sure that you are not neglecting your relationships with them in order to focus on your business. It's also important to make time for family and friends, and to maintain open and honest communication with them about your business and the demands it places on your time and energy.

In conclusion, maintaining a healthy work-life balance is an essential part of running a successful consulting business. By setting clear boundaries, prioritizing self-care, delegating responsibilities, and being mindful of the impact your work has on your personal relationships, you can ensure that you are able to provide the best services to your clients while also maintaining your own wellbeing.

Chapter 21

Building a Strong Online Presence

As a consulting business owner, it's important to have a strong online presence. This will not only help you reach potential clients, but it will also give you a platform to showcase your expertise and build your brand. With so many people spending a significant amount of time online, having a well-established online presence can make all the difference when it comes to attracting new clients and building a successful business. In this chapter, we'll explore the best ways to build a strong online presence and connect with your target audience.

Why is a strong online presence important for your consulting business?

A strong online presence is essential for any business in today's digital age. It helps you reach a wider audience, build your brand, and showcase your expertise. For consulting businesses, a strong online presence can be especially beneficial as it allows you to:

- Reach potential clients: By having an online presence, you can reach a wider audience of potential clients who may not have heard of you otherwise. This can include those who live outside of your local area, or those who may not have come across your business in their usual search for consulting services.

- Build your brand: Your online presence is an opportunity to build and establish your brand. By creating a strong online presence, you can showcase your expertise and create a positive image of your business. This can help build trust and credibility with potential clients and help you stand out in a competitive market.

- Showcase your expertise: Your online presence can be used to showcase your expertise and knowledge in your field. By creating blog posts, articles, and other types of content, you can demonstrate your expertise and establish yourself as a thought leader in your industry.

How to build a strong online presence for your consulting business

Building a strong online presence for your consulting business is a process that takes time and effort, but it's well worth it in the long run. Here are some of the best ways to build a strong online presence for your consulting business:

1. Create a website: Your website is the foundation of your online presence. It's where potential clients will go to find out more about your business and what you have to offer. Your website should be professional, well-designed, and easy to navigate. It should include information about your business, your services, and your team, as well as a way for potential clients to get in touch with you.

2. Establish a blog: Blogging is a great way to establish yourself as an expert in your field and showcase your knowledge. By creating blog posts on topics related to your consulting services, you can demonstrate your expertise and build a following of potential clients.

3. Utilize social media: Social media is a great way to connect with your target audience and reach a wider audience of potential clients. Choose the platforms that are most relevant to your target audience and use them to share information about your business, your services, and your expertise.

4. Optimize for search engines: To ensure that your website and other online content is easily discoverable, you need to optimize it for search engines. This means using keywords, meta descriptions, and other strategies to help search engines understand what your content is about and rank it appropriately.

5. Collaborate with others: Collaborating with other businesses and individuals in your industry can help you reach a wider audience and build your online presence. For example, you could guest post on other blogs, participate in online forums, or contribute to industry publications.

There are several benefits to having a strong online presence for your consulting business. First, it increases your visibility and reach, making it easier for potential clients to find and connect with you. Second, it helps you build credibility and establish yourself as an expert in your niche. Third, it allows you to showcase your services and past work, giving potential clients a better understanding of what you can offer. Finally, it provides you with a platform to interact with clients and prospects, helping to build strong relationships and increase conversions.

Building Your Website

Your website is the cornerstone of your online presence and serves as a virtual storefront for your business. To build a strong website, it's important to have a clear, user-friendly design, informative content, and a simple and straightforward navigation. You'll also want to make sure your website is optimized for search engines, so it can easily be found by potential clients.

Social Media

Social media is another important aspect of building a strong online presence. Platforms like Twitter, Facebook, Instagram, and LinkedIn are excellent ways to connect with potential clients and build your brand. By regularly posting content, engaging with followers, and leveraging paid advertising options, you can increase your visibility and reach online.

Blogging

Blogging is another excellent way to establish yourself as an expert in your niche and build your online presence. By creating and publishing blog articles on topics related to your consulting services, you can position yourself as a thought leader in your industry and attract potential clients.

Online Marketing

Finally, online marketing can help you reach a wider audience and build a strong online presence for your consulting business. From pay-per-click advertising to email marketing, there are several options available to help you drive traffic to your website and increase conversions.

Conclusion

Having a strong online presence is crucial for the success of your consulting business in today's digital age. By building a website, utilizing social media, blogging, and online marketing, you can increase your visibility, build credibility, and connect with potential clients. So don't wait, start building your online presence today and see the results for yourself!

Chapter 22

Managing Your Reputation

As a consultant, your reputation is everything. It's what sets you apart from your competitors, and it's what helps you win new business. Your reputation is built on the quality of your work, your interactions with clients, and your overall professional demeanor. That's why it's so important to manage your reputation carefully and intentionally, especially in today's digital age.

One of the most powerful tools you have at your disposal for managing your reputation is online reviews. Many potential clients will do a quick search online before deciding whether or not to work with you, and they'll be looking for reviews from other people who have worked with you in the past. If your reviews are positive, it can be a huge boost to your reputation and your business. On the other hand, if your reviews are negative, it can be devastating to your bottom line.

To ensure that your online reviews are positive, it's important to provide excellent customer service to all of your clients. Make sure that you listen to their concerns, respond promptly to any questions or issues they may have, and go above and beyond to make sure that they're satisfied with the services you provide. Additionally, consider offering incentives for clients to leave positive reviews, such as discounts on future services or gifts.

In addition to online reviews, there are a number of other strategies you can use to manage your reputation. For example:

- Maintain a strong online presence. Make sure that you have a professional website and a strong social media presence. This can help you build your reputation and reach new clients.

- Network regularly. Attend industry events, join professional organizations, and connect with other consultants in your field. This can help you build relationships with potential clients and colleagues, and it can also give you valuable opportunities to promote your business and your services.

- Stay up-to-date with industry trends. By staying informed about the latest developments in your field, you can position yourself as an expert and a thought leader in your industry. This can help you build your reputation and increase your credibility.

- Be honest and transparent. If something goes wrong or you make a mistake, be upfront about it and work to rectify the situation as quickly as possible. Being transparent and honest can help you build trust with your clients and maintain your reputation.

Managing your reputation is an ongoing process, but by following these tips, you can ensure that your reputation remains strong and that you continue to build a successful consulting business. By focusing on providing excellent customer service, networking regularly, and staying informed about the latest industry trends, you can establish yourself as a trusted and respected consultant in your field.

Chapter 23.

Growing Your Business

Starting your own consulting business can be a challenging and rewarding experience, but it's important to remember that the journey doesn't end once you've established your brand and built a strong client base. In order to continue your success, you'll need to focus on growing your business and expanding your reach.

There are several key strategies you can use to grow your consulting business, including:

1. Diversifying Your Services: As your business grows, you may find that you want to expand the types of services you offer to your clients. This could mean adding new areas of expertise, such as working with a different industry or offering new types of consulting services.

2. Building Stronger Relationships with Existing Clients: Your existing clients are your best source of new business, so it's important to build strong relationships with them. This could mean reaching out to them regularly, staying in touch with their needs, and offering new and improved services.

3. Expanding Your Network: The more people you know in your industry, the more likely you are to hear about new opportunities and potential clients. Attend industry events, join professional organizations, and make connections through social media to build your network and grow your business.

4. Utilizing Marketing and Advertising: Investing in marketing and advertising is a great way to reach new clients and promote your business. This could include advertising in relevant industry publications, developing a strong online presence, and utilizing social media to reach a wider audience.

5. Hiring Additional Staff: As your business grows, you may need to bring on additional staff to help you manage the increased workload. Hiring new employees can help you provide better service to your clients and take your business to the next level.

6. Offering Special Promotions and Deals: Offering special promotions and deals to your clients can be a great way to attract new business and reward your existing clients. This could include discounts on your services, limited-time offers, or special promotions.

7. Developing Strong Partnerships: Partnering with other businesses or organizations in your industry can be a great way to grow your business. This could mean working together on projects, offering joint services, or collaborating on marketing and advertising efforts.

By focusing on these strategies, you can continue to grow your consulting business and take it to the next level. Just remember, growth takes time and effort, so be patient and stay focused on your goals.

In conclusion, growing your consulting business is an ongoing process that requires effort, dedication, and a commitment to improvement. By utilizing the strategies outlined above, you can continue to build on your success and reach new heights in your career as a consultant.

Chapter 24

Staying Organized and Productive

Staying organized and productive is crucial to the success of your consulting business. With so many tasks to complete, appointments to keep, and emails to respond to, it can be easy to become overwhelmed. However, by implementing the right strategies, you can streamline your work and maintain your focus. In this chapter, we will discuss several tips and tools that can help you stay organized and productive.

First and foremost, prioritize your tasks. Make a to-do list each day, and prioritize your items based on their importance and urgency. This will help you ensure that you are focusing on the right tasks at the right time. You can also break larger tasks down into smaller, more manageable steps, which can help you stay motivated and on track.

Next, use technology to your advantage. There are many productivity tools available, such as calendars, email management software, project management tools, and more. These tools can help you manage your time more effectively, keep track of deadlines, and communicate with your clients and team members. Some popular options include Trello, Asana, and Google Calendar.

Another key aspect of staying organized and productive is staying on top of your email. It's easy for your inbox to become cluttered and overwhelming, but by taking the time to manage it, you can stay in control. Unsubscribe from emails that are not important, create folders to organize your messages, and try to respond to each email in a timely manner.

Time management is also an important factor in staying organized and productive. Make sure to set aside dedicated blocks of time for specific tasks, such as responding to emails, working on projects, and conducting research. By allocating specific blocks of time to these tasks, you can ensure that you are not wasting time switching between different tasks and that you are maximizing your productivity.

Finally, make sure to take breaks and prioritize your well-being. While it's important to be productive, it's also crucial to avoid burnout. Take breaks throughout the day, go for a walk, or simply step away from your computer for a few minutes. By taking care of yourself, you'll be able to work more effectively and maintain a healthy work-life balance.

In conclusion, staying organized and productive is essential to the success of your consulting business. By prioritizing your tasks, using technology to your advantage, staying on top of your email, managing your time effectively, and taking care of your well-being, you can maintain a focus and streamline your work. By doing so, you'll be able to deliver the best possible results to your clients and grow your business.

Chapter 25.

Building Strong Client Relationships

As a consultant, your clients are the lifeblood of your business. Without them, you have no business to run. That's why it's so important to build strong, lasting relationships with each and every one of your clients. By doing so, you'll not only ensure their satisfaction and continued business, but also create a network of loyal referrals who will help grow your business over time.

So, what exactly does it take to build strong client relationships? Let's take a look at some key tips and strategies.

1. Communication is key. Make sure you're regularly communicating with your clients, whether that's through email, phone, or in-person meetings. The more you stay in touch, the stronger your relationship will become.

2. Listen to their needs and concerns. Your clients will have specific needs and concerns that they want addressed. Make sure you're paying attention and doing everything you can to meet those needs.

3. Be reliable and trustworthy. Your clients need to know that they can count on you to deliver on your promises. Make sure you're always meeting deadlines and following through on commitments.

4. Provide excellent customer service. No matter what industry you're in, great customer service is always a

key factor in building strong relationships. Make sure you're providing your clients with the support and assistance they need, no matter what.

5. Be flexible and adaptable. No two clients are exactly alike, and you may need to adapt your approach to best meet their needs. Be willing to change and adjust your approach as needed to keep your clients happy and satisfied.

6. Get to know your clients on a personal level. The more you know about your clients, the stronger your relationship will become. Take the time to get to know them as people, not just clients.

7. Offer added value. By going above and beyond what's expected of you, you'll set yourself apart from other consultants and build strong, lasting relationships with your clients.

8. Keep them updated. Regular updates on your progress and the results you're delivering will help build trust and strengthen your relationship with your clients.

By following these tips and strategies, you'll be well on your way to building strong, lasting relationships with your clients. And remember, these relationships are not just important for your clients' satisfaction, but also for the continued growth and success of your business. So make them a top priority, and you'll be sure to reap the rewards in the long run.

Chapter 26.

Keeping Up with Competition

Starting and maintaining a successful consulting business can be challenging, especially with so much competition in the market. Keeping up with competition is crucial for the growth and sustainability of your business. In this chapter, we'll discuss some ways to stay ahead of the competition and keep your business thriving.

1. Know Your Competitors

The first step in staying ahead of the competition is to understand who your competitors are. This includes researching their strengths and weaknesses, as well as the services they offer and the target audience they serve. This information will give you a better understanding of the market and help you determine what sets your business apart from others.

2. Keep Up with Industry Trends

It's important to stay informed about the latest industry trends, including technological advancements and changes in customer preferences. Attend conferences, trade shows, and events to network with other professionals and learn about new and emerging trends in your field. Additionally, subscribe to trade publications and online resources to stay up-to-date on the latest industry news and developments.

3. Offer Unique Services

To stand out from the competition, you need to offer services that are unique and set your business apart. For example, if you specialize in marketing consulting, you could focus on offering social media marketing services that your competitors don't offer. By offering unique services, you'll be able to differentiate yourself from your competitors and appeal to a wider range of customers.

4. Build Strong Relationships with Clients

Building strong relationships with clients is another way to stay ahead of the competition. By providing excellent customer service and forming strong partnerships with clients, you'll be able to retain clients and attract new ones. Additionally, word-of-mouth referrals from satisfied clients can be a valuable source of new business.

5. Continuously Innovate

Finally, it's important to continuously innovate and improve your services. This can include updating your skills and knowledge, investing in new technology, and staying ahead of the curve in terms of the latest industry trends. By continuously innovating, you'll be able to provide better services and stay ahead of the competition.

In conclusion, staying ahead of the competition is an ongoing process that requires continuous effort and attention. By knowing your competitors, staying up-to-date with industry trends, offering unique services, building strong relationships with clients, and continuously innovating, you'll be able to stay ahead of the competition and keep your consulting business thriving.

Chapter 27.

Expanding Your Services

As your consulting business grows and becomes more established, it may be time to consider expanding your services to reach new clients and markets. Whether you want to broaden your services to reach new audiences or offer a wider range of solutions to existing clients, expanding your services can be a great way to increase your revenue, reputation, and reach.

Before you start expanding your services, it's important to assess your current offerings and make sure you have the capacity and resources to handle more clients and projects. You may need to hire additional staff, invest in new technology, or upgrade your office space to accommodate your expanding business.

Once you've evaluated your resources, it's time to start considering what new services you can offer. Here are a few suggestions to get you started:

1. Specialize in a new area: If you have expertise in a particular area of consulting, consider specializing in that area to become an expert in the field. This will help you stand out from your competitors and attract new clients.

2. Offer new solutions: Consider what new solutions you can offer your clients, such as new technologies or innovative strategies. By staying ahead of the curve,

you'll be better equipped to meet the changing needs of your clients and stand out in your field.

3. Partner with other businesses: Partnering with other businesses in related fields can help you expand your services and reach new clients. For example, if you're a marketing consultant, you could partner with a web design firm to offer complete marketing and web design packages.

4. Expand your reach: Consider expanding your reach to new geographic locations or target markets. This could include opening a new office in another city or offering your services to new industries or demographics.

When expanding your services, it's important to ensure that your new offerings are in line with your brand and mission. Make sure that you're offering services that you're passionate about and that align with your goals and values. Additionally, be sure to communicate your new offerings clearly and effectively to your existing clients and potential clients through your website, marketing materials, and other channels.

Finally, be prepared for a potential learning curve as you expand your services. You may need to invest in additional training or education to stay current with new technologies or industry trends. However, with hard work, dedication, and a commitment to your clients, you can successfully expand your services and take your consulting business to the next level.

Chapter 28

Building a Strong Referral Network

As a consultant, your reputation is everything. One of the best ways to grow your business is through word-of-mouth referrals from happy clients. Not only does this save you time and resources on marketing and advertising, but it also helps establish trust with potential clients. In this chapter, we'll explore how to build a strong referral network for your consulting business.

Start with a Strong Base

Before you can start building a referral network, you need to make sure you have a solid foundation to work from. This means providing excellent service to your current clients and going above and beyond their expectations. If your clients are happy with the work you do, they'll be more likely to refer you to others.

Focus on Relationships

Building a referral network is all about building relationships. You want to develop strong connections with your clients so they feel comfortable recommending you to others. This means taking the time to get to know them, understanding their needs, and communicating regularly. You can also strengthen your relationships by being responsive and accessible, and by providing helpful resources and information.

Incentivize Referrals

Another way to encourage referrals is by offering incentives. This could be a discount on future services, a referral bonus, or even a gift card. Just make sure the incentive is something your clients will value and that it aligns with your business goals.

Ask for Referrals

Don't be afraid to ask for referrals! This is a simple and effective way to get the word out about your business. After a successful project, ask your client if they know anyone who could benefit from your services. You can also send out a follow-up email after a project is completed, asking if they know anyone who needs your help.

Networking

Networking is another great way to build a referral network. Attend events and conferences in your industry and make connections with other professionals. You never know who might refer you to a potential client or who might be in need of your services.

Stay in Touch

Staying in touch with your clients and referral network is essential to maintaining strong relationships. Regular communication helps keep your business top of mind and strengthens the bonds you've built. You can do this by sending regular newsletters, following up after projects, and reaching out just to check in.

Building a strong referral network takes time and effort, but the rewards are well worth it. By providing excellent service and developing strong relationships, you'll be able to grow your business and establish a positive reputation in your industry. So don't be afraid to reach out and ask for referrals - your business will thank you!

Chapter 29.

Diversifying Your Business

As a business owner, it's important to always be thinking ahead and looking for new ways to grow and expand your offerings. Diversifying your business can help mitigate risk, tap into new markets, and increase your revenue streams.

The first step in diversifying your business is to assess your current offerings and identify areas where you can expand. This can be done by analyzing your customer base, the services they are looking for, and the market trends in your industry. You can also ask for feedback from your current clients to see if there are any additional services they would like to see from your company.

Once you have a clear understanding of the areas where you can expand, it's time to start brainstorming new offerings that complement your current services. It's important to choose services that align with your core competencies and skills, and that you can deliver with the same level of quality as your current offerings. For example, if you're a marketing consultant, you could expand into web design or content creation.

When launching new services, it's important to carefully plan and research your market to ensure that there is demand for the new offerings. This can include market surveys, focus groups, and competitor analysis. You should also take into account the resources and costs associated with launching the new services, including staffing, equipment, and marketing expenses.

Once you have a clear plan in place, it's time to start promoting your new offerings to your current and potential customers. This can be done through email marketing, social media, and networking events. It's important to communicate the benefits of the new services, and how they complement your current offerings.

In order to successfully diversify your business, you will also need to invest in the necessary training and resources for your employees. This can include attending industry conferences, enrolling in online courses, and hiring experts in the field.

It's also important to continuously monitor the success of your new offerings and make adjustments as needed. This can include adjusting your pricing, marketing strategies, and the services themselves based on customer feedback and market trends.

Diversifying your business can be a great way to increase your revenue streams, tap into new markets, and mitigate risk. However, it's important to approach diversification with careful planning and research, and to continuously monitor and adjust your offerings based on market trends and customer feedback.

In conclusion, diversifying your business is a smart strategy for growth and success. By expanding your offerings and tapping into new markets, you can increase your revenue streams and establish your business as a leader in your industry. With careful planning and research, and a commitment to continuous improvement, you can successfully diversify your business and take your company to the next level.

Chapter 30.

Utilizing Social Media and Online Marketing

Social media and online marketing are essential components of a successful consulting business. In today's digital age, having a strong online presence is critical for reaching new clients, building brand awareness, and showcasing your expertise. Whether you're a startup or an established firm, utilizing social media and online marketing can help you reach new heights of success.

There are many different social media platforms available to businesses, each with its own unique benefits. For example, LinkedIn is a great platform for connecting with other professionals, sharing industry news, and showcasing your expertise. Twitter can be used for real-time updates, engaging with followers, and building brand awareness. Instagram is a great platform for visual storytelling, showcasing your brand personality, and connecting with customers.

When it comes to online marketing, there are a variety of tactics you can use to reach new clients. Search engine optimization (SEO) involves optimizing your website and online content so that it ranks higher in search engine results. Pay-per-click advertising (PPC) involves creating online ads that only appear when someone searches for a specific keyword. Content marketing involves creating valuable, relevant content that engages your target audience and helps you establish your expertise in your niche.

Before you begin your online marketing efforts, it's important to have a clear understanding of your target audience. Who are you trying to reach, and what do they care about? What are their pain points, and how can you help solve them? This understanding will help you create content and social media strategies that resonate with your target audience and help you reach your goals.

To maximize the impact of your social media and online marketing efforts, it's important to be consistent and strategic. Choose a set of platforms that make sense for your business, and use them regularly to share updates, connect with followers, and build your brand. When it comes to online marketing, it's important to have a clear strategy in place, including specific goals, tactics, and metrics for measuring success.

If you're just getting started with social media and online marketing, it can be helpful to work with a professional who can help you get up and running quickly. A good digital marketing agency can help you create a strategy that aligns with your goals, optimizes your online presence, and drives traffic to your website.

In conclusion, social media and online marketing are essential components of a successful consulting business. Whether you're just getting started or looking to expand your reach, utilizing these tools can help you connect with new clients, build brand awareness, and achieve your goals. Just be sure to have a clear understanding of your target audience, be consistent and strategic, and work with the right professionals to help you succeed.

Chapter 31

Creating a Strong Marketing Plan

Marketing is the key to growing your business and reaching new customers. A solid marketing plan will help you identify your target audience, communicate your value proposition, and measure your success. In this chapter, we will cover the steps you need to take to create a strong marketing plan that will help you achieve your business goals.

Step 1: Define Your Target Audience

The first step in creating a marketing plan is to determine your target audience. This is the group of people who are most likely to be interested in your products or services. Understanding your target audience will help you tailor your marketing efforts to their specific needs and interests. To define your target audience, consider the following factors:

- Age

- Gender

- Income

- Location

- Occupation

- Hobbies and interests

Once you have a clear understanding of your target audience, you can tailor your marketing efforts to their specific needs and interests. For example, if your target audience is young professionals in their 20s and 30s, you may want to focus your marketing efforts on social media platforms like Instagram and Facebook.

Step 2: Determine Your Unique Selling Proposition (USP)

Your Unique Selling Proposition (USP) is what sets your business apart from your competition. It is what makes your products or services unique and valuable to your target audience. To determine your USP, consider the following:

- What sets your business apart from your competition?

- What are the benefits of your products or services?

- What makes your products or services unique and valuable to your target audience?

Once you have determined your USP, you can use it to create a clear and compelling marketing message that will help you reach your target audience and convert them into customers.

Step 3: Create a Marketing Mix

Your marketing mix is the combination of tactics you will use to reach your target audience and achieve your marketing goals. There are four key components of the marketing mix:

- Product: This includes the products or services you offer and how they meet the needs and wants of your target audience.

- Price: This includes the price you charge for your products or services and how it compares to your competition.

- Place: This includes the channels you use to distribute your products or services, such as online or in-store.

- Promotion: This includes the methods you use to communicate your marketing message, such as advertising, public relations, and sales promotions.

When creating your marketing mix, it is important to consider the needs and wants of your target audience, your USP, and your budget. The goal is to create a balanced mix of tactics that will help you reach your target audience and achieve your marketing goals.

Step 4: Set Marketing Goals and Objectives

Before you start your marketing efforts, it is important to set clear marketing goals and objectives. Your marketing goals should be specific, measurable, and achievable. For example, if your goal is to increase website traffic, you might set the objective of increasing website traffic by 20% in the next six months.

Step 5: Measure Your Results

The final step in creating a strong marketing plan is to measure your results. This will help you determine which tactics are working well and which tactics need to be adjusted. There are several metrics you can use to measure your marketing success, including:

- Website traffic

- Lead generation

- Sales

- Return on investment (ROI)

By measuring your results, you can continually improve your marketing efforts and achieve your marketing goals.

In conclusion, creating a strong marketing plan is a crucial step in the success of your business. By understanding your target audience, defining your unique selling points, and setting realistic goals, you can develop a strategy that effectively promotes your brand and grows your business. A well-executed marketing plan can help you reach your target customers, increase brand recognition, and ultimately drive more sales.

However, it is important to remember that a marketing plan is not a one-time project, but rather an ongoing effort. Regularly revisiting and adjusting your plan as needed can ensure that it stays relevant and effective in a constantly changing market. With the right combination of creativity, strategy, and hard work, you can build a marketing plan that takes your business to new heights.

Chapter 32

Building Relationships with Industry Leaders

Building relationships with industry leaders is a crucial step in growing your business and establishing yourself as a leader in your field. These relationships can provide valuable resources, knowledge, and exposure to new opportunities. In this chapter, we will discuss the importance of building relationships with industry leaders and provide tips on how to make it happen.

Why build relationships with industry leaders? Industry leaders are often the pioneers of their field and have a wealth of experience and knowledge to share. They can provide insights into emerging trends, new technologies, and business strategies that you may not have considered. Building relationships with these leaders can help you stay ahead of the curve and stay informed about the latest developments in your industry.

In addition to their expertise, industry leaders can also provide valuable referrals, mentorship, and connections to other professionals in your field. These relationships can lead to new business opportunities, collaborations, and partnerships that can help you grow your business.

How to build relationships with industry leaders

1. Attend events and conferences: One of the best ways to meet industry leaders is to attend events and

conferences where they will be speaking or participating. This provides an opportunity to meet them in person and engage with them on a more personal level.

2. Connect online: Utilize social media and professional networking sites to connect with industry leaders. Follow their accounts, engage with their posts, and share your own relevant content. You can also reach out to them directly to start a conversation or ask for advice.

3. Read their work: Industry leaders often publish articles, books, or blog posts about their experiences and insights. Read their work and share your thoughts on their ideas. This will demonstrate your interest and knowledge in their work, and may lead to a conversation.

4. Offer value: When reaching out to industry leaders, be sure to offer value to them. This could be in the form of an introduction to someone in their network, helpful information, or a thoughtful contribution to a discussion. By demonstrating your value, you increase the likelihood that they will be interested in building a relationship with you.

5. Be genuine: Building relationships with industry leaders requires authenticity and genuine interest in their work and ideas. Avoid being overly pushy or trying to sell them something. Instead, focus on building a relationship based on mutual respect and shared interests.

6. Follow up: After meeting an industry leader, be sure to follow up with them. Send a thoughtful email or connect with them on social media. Keep the conversation going and continue to offer value.

By building relationships with industry leaders, you can expand your network, gain valuable insights, and grow your business. Remember to be genuine, offer value, and be persistent in your efforts. With time and effort, you can establish yourself as a leader in your field and reap the rewards of these important relationships.

Chapter 33.

Becoming an Authority in Your Field

As a business owner, establishing yourself as an authority in your field is crucial to your success. Not only will it help you stand out from the competition, but it will also attract new clients, increase your credibility, and give you a sense of pride and accomplishment. In this chapter, we'll discuss what it means to be an authority in your field and how you can achieve this status.

What Does it Mean to be an Authority?

Being an authority in your field means that you are recognized as an expert in your industry. People in your field look to you for guidance, advice, and information, and you are respected for your knowledge and experience. When people think of your area of expertise, they associate your name with it.

How to Become an Authority in Your Field

Becoming an authority in your field takes time, effort, and dedication. Here are some steps you can take to achieve this status:

1. Focus on a specific niche: Instead of trying to be an expert in a broad range of topics, focus on a specific niche within your field. This will allow you to build deeper knowledge and expertise, and make it easier for people to recognize you as an authority in your specific area.

2. Stay up-to-date with industry trends: Keep yourself informed of the latest developments in your field by reading industry publications, attending conferences, and participating in online forums and groups. The more you know, the more valuable you will be as an authority.

3. Share your knowledge: One of the best ways to establish yourself as an authority is to share your knowledge and expertise with others. Write articles and blog posts, speak at conferences and events, and engage in online discussions. The more you share, the more your reputation will grow.

4. Network with industry leaders: Building relationships with other leaders in your field will help you expand your knowledge and gain valuable insights into the industry. Attend industry events, join professional organizations, and participate in online communities.

5. Provide value: When you provide value to others in your field, you demonstrate your expertise and gain recognition as an authority. Offer to speak at events, mentor others, and provide helpful advice and resources.

6. Build your online presence: Establishing a strong online presence is essential in today's world. Create a professional website, engage with others on social media, and participate in online forums and groups. The more you participate, the more people will recognize you as an authority.

7. Demonstrate your expertise: Share case studies and examples of your work, and let your results speak for themselves. The more you demonstrate your expertise, the more people will trust and respect you as an authority.

Conclusion

Becoming an authority in your field takes time, effort, and dedication, but the rewards are well worth it. When you are recognized as an expert in your industry, you will enjoy increased credibility, a sense of pride, and a steady stream of new clients. By focusing on your niche, staying up-to-date with industry trends, sharing your knowledge, networking with industry leaders, providing value, building your online presence, and demonstrating your expertise, you can achieve the status of an authority in your field.

Chapter 34.

Keeping Your Business Ethical

Starting and running a business can be exciting and rewarding, but it's also important to ensure that you are conducting business in an ethical and responsible manner. Not only will this help you build a good reputation, but it will also give you peace of mind knowing that you are making a positive impact on the world.

What is Business Ethics?

Business ethics refers to the moral principles and values that guide the behavior of a business. These principles include honesty, fairness, and respect for people and the environment. When a business operates ethically, it creates a culture of trust and integrity that attracts customers, employees, and partners.

Why is Business Ethics Important?

There are many reasons why it's important to practice good business ethics. Firstly, ethical businesses are more likely to build long-lasting relationships with their customers and partners. Customers are more likely to return to businesses that they trust, and partners are more likely to recommend a business that operates with integrity.

Another reason why business ethics is important is because it helps protect the reputation of a business. A business with a good reputation is more likely to attract new customers and retain existing ones. In contrast, a business with a negative reputation is likely to lose customers and face difficulty attracting new business.

Finally, practicing good business ethics is simply the right thing to do. It helps ensure that businesses are contributing to a better world, and that they are making a positive impact on the people and communities they serve.

How to Ensure Your Business is Ethical

Here are a few steps you can take to ensure that your business operates in an ethical manner:

1. Establish a Code of Conduct: Developing a code of conduct is a good first step in ensuring that your business operates ethically. Your code of conduct should outline the values and principles that your business stands for, and it should be communicated to all employees and partners.

2. Train Employees: Once you have established your code of conduct, it's important to train your employees on what it means and how to put it into practice. This will help ensure that everyone is on the same page and that everyone is working towards the same goal.

3. Monitor Your Supply Chain: It's important to monitor your supply chain to ensure that the products and services you offer are ethically sourced. This means that you should ensure that your suppliers are not engaging in practices such as child labor, forced labor, or environmental degradation.

4. Practice Transparency: Being transparent about your business practices is a key aspect of operating ethically. This means being open and honest about your business practices and making it easy for customers and partners to find information about your business.

5. Address Ethical Issues: Finally, it's important to address ethical issues when they arise. This means being proactive in addressing problems, and taking steps to prevent similar problems from happening in the future.

In conclusion, keeping your business ethical is essential to its success and longevity. By following the steps outlined above, you can ensure that your business is operating in an ethical and responsible manner, and that it is making a positive impact on the world. By operating ethically, you'll be able to build strong relationships with your customers, employees, and partners, and you'll be able to sleep well at night knowing that you are doing the right thing.

Chapter 35

Managing Client Expectations

Managing client expectations is an essential part of running a successful business. When clients have realistic and well-communicated expectations, they are more likely to be satisfied with your services, leading to repeat business and positive reviews. On the other hand, if you don't effectively manage client expectations, it can result in frustration, dissatisfaction, and a tarnished reputation.

Here are some tips for effectively managing client expectations:

1. Clearly communicate your process: From the start of a project, it is crucial to outline your process and set expectations for how you work. This can include steps such as project timelines, check-ins, and how you will communicate progress. By clearly communicating your process, clients will understand what to expect from you and when.

2. Be transparent about your skills and limitations: It's important to be honest about your abilities and what you can deliver. If you can't fulfill a client's request, it's better to say so early on and find a solution together rather than trying to deliver something that falls short of their expectations.

3. Regular check-ins and updates: Regular check-ins and updates help keep clients informed and informed of the progress of their project. It also provides opportunities

to address any concerns or make any necessary adjustments to meet expectations.

4. Be responsive and proactive: Responding promptly to client inquiries and being proactive in addressing any concerns can help build trust and satisfaction. It's important to listen to your clients and be open to feedback, taking any necessary actions to resolve any issues.

5. Keep expectations realistic: While it's important to strive to meet and exceed client expectations, it's also crucial to keep expectations realistic. Setting unattainable expectations can result in disappointment and dissatisfaction, so it's essential to be honest about what is possible and what is not.

6. Document everything: Keeping detailed records of conversations, agreements, and deliverables can help avoid misunderstandings and ensure everyone is on the same page. This documentation can also be used to reference later if any questions or concerns arise.

7. Be open to feedback and adjust as needed: Feedback from clients can be valuable in helping you understand what you're doing well and where there is room for improvement. Be open to constructive criticism and take any necessary actions to address any concerns and meet expectations.

In conclusion, managing client expectations is a critical part of running a successful business. By clearly communicating your process, being transparent about your skills and limitations, staying responsive and proactive, keeping expectations realistic, documenting everything, and being open to feedback, you can help ensure your clients are satisfied and continue to do business with you.

Chapter 36.

Staying Focused on Your Goals

Starting and growing a successful business takes a lot of hard work, dedication, and focus. It's easy to get sidetracked by the many responsibilities and tasks that come with running a business, but it's important to stay focused on your goals and make sure that every decision you make is in line with your long-term vision. In this chapter, we'll explore ways to stay focused on your goals and stay motivated as you work towards success.

Define Your Goals

The first step to staying focused on your goals is to make sure that you have a clear understanding of what those goals are. This might include things like increasing your revenue, expanding your services, growing your customer base, or improving your brand recognition. Write your goals down and make sure that you have a clear understanding of what success looks like for each one. This will help you stay focused on what's important and make sure that you're working towards your vision.

Set Specific, Measurable, Achievable, Relevant, and Time-bound (SMART) Goals

Once you have defined your goals, it's important to make sure that they are specific, measurable, achievable, relevant, and time-bound (SMART). This will help you stay focused on what you need to do to achieve your goals and make sure that you're making progress.

For example, if your goal is to increase your revenue, you might set a SMART goal to increase your sales by 10% over the next six months. This goal is specific (increase sales), measurable (by 10%), achievable (with hard work and a solid marketing plan), relevant (to your business's success), and time-bound (over the next six months).

Stay Motivated

Staying focused on your goals can be challenging, especially when you're faced with obstacles or setbacks. That's why it's important to stay motivated and find ways to stay inspired as you work towards your vision.

One way to stay motivated is to surround yourself with positive, supportive people who believe in you and your business. Surround yourself with friends and family members who encourage you and offer words of support when you need it. You can also join a business support group or attend networking events to connect with like-minded individuals who are facing similar challenges.

Another way to stay motivated is to find inspiration in the success of others. Read success stories, watch TED Talks, or listen to podcasts from entrepreneurs and business leaders who have overcome obstacles and achieved their goals. These stories can help you stay focused on your vision and keep pushing forward when things get tough.

Celebrate Your Wins

Finally, make sure to celebrate your wins along the way. No matter how small the accomplishment, it's important to take time to acknowledge your progress and celebrate your successes. This will help you stay motivated and focused on your goals, and it will give you the energy and enthusiasm you need to keep pushing forward.

In conclusion, staying focused on your goals is a crucial aspect of running a successful business. By setting clear and achievable goals, regularly reviewing and adjusting your plan, and keeping yourself accountable, you can stay on track and reach your desired outcomes. Furthermore, staying focused on your goals helps you prioritize your time and resources, remain motivated, and avoid distractions and setbacks.

However, it's also important to be flexible and open-minded. Your goals may change over time, and you may need to make adjustments to your plan. This is okay and a normal part of the process. The key is to stay focused on what's important to you and your business and continue working towards your goals, no matter what challenges you may face.

In the end, staying focused on your goals is a key component of success in business and in life. It requires discipline, hard work, and a positive attitude, but the rewards are well worth it. So, keep your eyes on the prize and stay focused on your goals, and you'll surely achieve the success you desire.

Chapter 37

Developing a Strong Work Culture

As a business owner, you are the primary driver of the work culture in your company. The work culture is a critical aspect of any organization, and it can have a significant impact on employee morale, productivity, and overall business success. A positive work culture can make employees feel valued and motivated to do their best work, while a negative work culture can lead to high turnover rates and low morale.

To develop a strong work culture, you need to focus on creating an environment that is supportive, inclusive, and respectful. Here are some key strategies that you can implement to create a positive work culture:

1. Clearly define your values and mission: Your values and mission should be at the center of your work culture. This will help you make decisions that align with your company's goals and purpose, and it will also help employees understand the company's priorities. Make sure that your values and mission are communicated clearly to all employees, and that they are reflected in the way that you do business.

2. Encourage open communication: Encourage open communication by creating a safe and supportive environment where employees feel comfortable sharing their thoughts and ideas. This can be achieved through regular team meetings, regular one-on-one meetings with employees, and through open and transparent feedback systems.

3. Promote a healthy work-life balance: Make sure that employees have a healthy work-life balance by offering flexible working arrangements, and by encouraging employees to take time off when they need it. This can help to reduce stress and increase job satisfaction, and it can also improve productivity.

4. Foster collaboration and teamwork: Encourage collaboration and teamwork by creating opportunities for employees to work together on projects and by providing resources that support collaboration. This can help to build strong relationships between employees and improve overall productivity.

5. Recognize and reward employees: Recognize and reward employees for their hard work and achievements. This can be done through performance-based bonuses, promotions, and public recognition. This will help to boost employee morale and motivation, and it will also show employees that their contributions are valued.

6. Invest in employee training and development: Investing in employee training and development can help to improve employee skills, increase job satisfaction, and foster a sense of personal and professional growth. Offer opportunities for employees to attend training sessions, conferences, and workshops, and provide resources for employees to continue their learning and professional development.

7. Create a supportive and inclusive environment: Create a supportive and inclusive environment by promoting diversity and equality, and by encouraging employees

to bring their unique perspectives and experiences to work. This can help to create a more dynamic and innovative work culture, and it will also help to build stronger relationships between employees.

In conclusion, building a strong work culture is essential for the success of your business. By focusing on creating a supportive, inclusive, and respectful environment, you can improve employee morale, boost productivity, and foster a positive and dynamic work culture. By investing in employee training and development, encouraging collaboration and teamwork, and promoting a healthy work-life balance, you can create an environment where employees feel valued and motivated to do their best work.

Chapter 38

Maintaining a Growth Mindset

As a business owner or entrepreneur, it's important to always have a growth mindset. This means that you are always seeking new opportunities and ways to improve yourself, your business, and your industry. A growth mindset can help you stay motivated, confident, and focused on your goals, even when things get tough. In this chapter, we'll explore how to maintain a growth mindset and how it can benefit you and your business.

What is a Growth Mindset?

A growth mindset is a way of thinking that embraces challenges and views mistakes as opportunities to learn and grow. Instead of focusing on what they can't do, individuals with a growth mindset focus on what they can do and how they can improve. This mindset is characterized by a desire to learn, an open-mindedness to new ideas, and a resilience in the face of setbacks.

Benefits of Maintaining a Growth Mindset

There are many benefits to maintaining a growth mindset, including:

1. Improved performance: People with a growth mindset tend to perform better in their personal and professional lives. They are more likely to take on challenging tasks and to see failures as opportunities to learn and grow, rather than as reasons to give up.

2. Increased creativity: A growth mindset encourages you to think outside the box and to see problems from different perspectives. This can lead to more creative and innovative solutions, which can give you an edge in a competitive market.

3. Greater resilience: When you have a growth mindset, you are better able to handle stress and setbacks. You view setbacks as opportunities to learn, grow, and improve, rather than as reasons to give up.

4. Better relationships: A growth mindset can also help you build stronger relationships with others. When you are open-minded and willing to learn from others, you are more likely to form positive and productive relationships with colleagues, clients, and customers.

How to Maintain a Growth Mindset

1. Embrace challenges: Rather than viewing challenges as obstacles, see them as opportunities to grow and improve. This will help you stay motivated and focused on your goals, even when things get tough.

2. Stay curious: Keep an open mind and be curious about the world around you. Ask questions, seek out new information, and explore new ideas. This will help you see things from different perspectives and broaden your understanding of your industry and your business.

3. Learn from failures: Instead of dwelling on failures, use them as opportunities to learn and grow. Ask yourself what you can do differently next time, and use this

information to make improvements in your personal and professional life.

4. Surround yourself with positive people: Surround yourself with people who support your growth and development. Seek out mentors and build relationships with individuals who can help you grow and succeed.

5. Celebrate your successes: Celebrate your successes, no matter how small they may be. Acknowledge your achievements and take the time to reflect on what you've learned and how you've grown.

6. Stay flexible: Be open to change and be willing to adapt your approach as needed. This will help you stay responsive to changes in your industry and in your business, and will help you continue to grow and improve.

Conclusion

Having a growth mindset is essential for success as a business owner or entrepreneur. By embracing challenges, staying curious, learning from failures, and celebrating your successes, you can maintain a growth mindset and continue to grow and improve. Remember, a growth mindset is not just about achieving your goals, it's about enjoying the journey and becoming the best version of yourself. So, be open to new ideas

Chapter 39

Staying Adaptable and Resilient

Starting and running a successful business can be a roller coaster ride of ups and downs. The key to success is not only having a great product or service, but also being able to adapt to changes in the market and maintain resilience when faced with challenges. In this chapter, we will explore the importance of staying adaptable and resilient as a business owner.

Why Staying Adaptable is Critical for Business Success

The business landscape is constantly changing. New technologies emerge, customer needs evolve, and competitors enter the market. In order to succeed, you must be able to adapt to these changes and pivot your business strategy as necessary.

One of the biggest advantages of staying adaptable is that it allows you to stay ahead of the competition. By being proactive and anticipating changes in the market, you can stay ahead of your competitors and continue to grow your business.

For example, let's say that a new technology is introduced that could significantly impact your industry. By staying adaptable and being open to incorporating this technology into your business, you could have a competitive advantage over other businesses that are slow to adopt the new technology.

Staying Adaptable Helps You Avoid Burnout

Being able to adapt to change can also help you avoid burnout as a business owner. Running a business can be stressful and demanding, and it's important to find ways to manage that stress. By staying adaptable and being open to new ideas and approaches, you can find new and innovative ways to tackle challenges and reduce stress levels.

How to Maintain Resilience

Along with staying adaptable, it's also important to maintain resilience as a business owner. Resilience is the ability to bounce back from setbacks and challenges and keep moving forward. In order to maintain resilience, it's important to focus on the following:

1. Take care of yourself: It's important to prioritize self-care and make sure you're taking care of your physical, mental, and emotional well-being. This can include things like exercise, meditation, and spending time with loved ones.

2. Surround yourself with support: Having a strong support system can help you stay resilient during tough times. This can include friends, family, and mentors who can provide encouragement and guidance.

3. Keep perspective: When faced with challenges, it's important to maintain a big-picture perspective and focus on your goals. This will help you stay motivated and stay the course.

4. Embrace change: Instead of viewing change as a threat, embrace it as an opportunity for growth. This mindset

can help you be more resilient and better able to handle challenges.

5. Celebrate small wins: Celebrating small wins along the way can help you stay motivated and build momentum. Whether it's landing a new client or reaching a personal goal, taking the time to acknowledge and celebrate your successes can help you stay resilient and keep moving forward.

In conclusion, staying adaptable and maintaining resilience are critical for success in business. By being open to change, taking care of yourself, and embracing challenges as opportunities for growth, you can build a business that is not only successful, but also fulfilling and enjoyable.

Chapter 40.

Celebrating Your Success

Running a business can be a challenging and demanding endeavor, and it's essential to take time to recognize and celebrate your successes along the way. Celebrating your achievements helps to build a positive and motivated work culture, and it's a way to reward yourself and your team for the hard work and dedication that goes into growing and maintaining a successful business. In this chapter, we'll discuss the importance of celebrating your successes and how to do so in a meaningful way.

Why Celebrate Your Successes?

Celebrating your successes is an essential aspect of business management, and there are several reasons why it's so important. Firstly, it's a way to recognize the hard work and dedication that goes into running a successful business. Your employees, in particular, will appreciate the recognition and reward for their efforts, which can help to boost morale and motivation.

Celebrating your successes also provides an opportunity to reflect on your progress and growth as a business. By taking a moment to acknowledge your accomplishments, you can gain a better perspective on what's working well and what areas may need improvement. This self-reflection can lead to new insights and ideas for future growth and success.

In addition, celebrating your successes can help to build a positive work culture. By recognizing and rewarding success, you create a supportive and motivating environment where your employees feel valued and appreciated. This, in turn, can lead to higher levels of engagement and productivity, which is essential for long-term success.

How to Celebrate Your Successes

There are many different ways to celebrate your successes, and the best approach will depend on the size and type of your business, as well as the preferences of your employees. Here are some ideas to get you started:

1. Employee Recognition Programs: Implementing a formal recognition program can be a great way to celebrate the successes of your employees. This could be as simple as acknowledging an employee of the month, or it could involve a more elaborate reward system, such as a company trip or a monetary bonus.

2. Celebratory Events: Hosting a company-wide event, such as a picnic, a party or a team-building day, is a great way to celebrate your successes as a team. This provides an opportunity for employees to connect with one another, and it helps to build a strong sense of community and belonging within your workplace.

3. Employee Perks: Offering your employees special perks or privileges can be a great way to celebrate their successes. This could be as simple as offering them a flexible work schedule or additional time off, or it could involve offering a discounted gym membership or other wellness benefits.

4. Community Outreach: Engaging in community outreach initiatives is a great way to celebrate your successes while giving back to your local community. This could involve volunteering at a local food bank, organizing a charity event, or supporting a local nonprofit organization.

5. Personalized Rewards: Personalized rewards, such as a handwritten note of gratitude, a special gift or a personalized experience, can be a powerful way to celebrate the successes of your employees. This helps to show your employees that their efforts are truly valued and appreciated.

Conclusion

Celebrating your successes is an essential aspect of business management, and it's important to take the time to recognize and reward your employees for their hard work and dedication. By celebrating your successes, you can help to build a positive work culture, gain new insights into your business, and motivate and engage your employees for long-term success. So take the time to celebrate your successes, and don't be afraid to get creative in the process!

As we come to the end of this book, we hope that you have found the information contained within to be helpful and informative. Running a business is never easy, but by following the tips and strategies outlined here, we believe that you can achieve great success and fulfillment in your entrepreneurial journey.

We know that the road to success can be long and challenging, but we encourage you to stay committed and persistent. Remember to stay focused on your goals, maintain a growth mindset, and remain adaptable and resilient in the face of challenges.

Never forget the importance of building strong relationships with your clients and partners, and of providing excellent customer service. We also hope that the chapters on building a strong online presence, developing a marketing plan, and utilizing technology and tools have helped you to leverage the power of digital platforms and marketing to grow your business.

Finally, we encourage you to celebrate your successes, no matter how big or small. Every accomplishment is a step towards building a successful and fulfilling business.

We wish you all the best on your entrepreneurial journey, and we hope that this book has been a valuable resource for you. Remember to stay focused, stay committed, and keep moving forward. Success is within reach, and we believe that you can achieve it.